Friendship
Psalms

Presented To:

Arlene

Presented By:

Messiah Women's Retreat

Date:

March 2-4, 2001

Friendship
Psalms

God's Gift

of Joy

and Encouragement

HONOR
BOOKS

Honor Books
Tulsa, Oklahoma

Friendship Psalms
ISBN 1-56292-833-3
Copyright © 2000 by GRQ Ink, Inc.
381 Riverside Drive, Suite 250
Franklin, Tennessee 37064

Published by Honor Books
P.O. Box 55388
Tulsa, Oklahoma 74155

Developed by GRQ Ink, Inc.
Manuscript written by Margaret Langstaff
Cover and text design by Richmond & Williams
Composition by Educational Publishing Concepts, Inc.

*I pray that the
LORD will listen
when you are in
trouble, and that
the God of Jacob
will keep you safe.*

PSALM 20:1 CEV

Friends Support Each Other

I come to you for shelter.
Protect me, keep me safe, and don't disappoint me.
PSALM 25:20 CEV

The phone rings as you are fixing supper. You have five minutes to get the casserole in the oven before you have to pick up the kids from ball practice. "Hi," a familiar voice says. "Can you talk?" You start to explain how hectic things are and ask if you can call back later, but something stops you—something in that familiar voice that isn't quite right. "Sure," you say, glancing at the kitchen clock. "What's up?"

And sure enough, the world is caving in on an old friend. She is at her wit's end. She has no one she can talk to about her problems, no one who understands and cares as much as you. Though you realize her problems cannot be solved in a single phone conversation, you know you can help lift her spirit by allowing her to reach out to you. Suddenly all of your priorities are rearranged. Nothing is more important at that instant than you "being there" for your friend.

God is our model for friendship. He is never too busy to hear our cries for help, never too distracted to reach out to us when we need Him.

Give ear, O Lord, to my prayer;
listen to my cry of supplication.
In the day of my trouble I call on you,
for you will answer me.

PSALM 86:6-7 NRSV

Friends Are Kind

I celebrate and shout because you are kind.
You saw all my suffering, and you cared for me.
PSALM 31:7 CEV

Two women went to lunch at a nice restaurant to celebrate one's recent promotion at work. The one who had received the promotion had struggled with hostile coworkers and a difficult boss. Through this dark period on the job, it seemed that no one appreciated her work. Credit for her accomplishments often went to her boss, who was only too eager to take the praise for himself. During those difficult months, she poured her heart out to her friend, who was always there to listen and to sympathize.

Now sitting in the restaurant with her loyal and long-suffering friend, she realized what a trial it must have been for her, too. All the whining and complaining must have nearly driven her crazy. Embarrassed and full of regret for having been a burden, she started to apologize. "Don't be silly," her friend said, interrupting. "You're like a sister to me."

The word "kind" is derived from "kin", which means "relative." We are sisters and brothers in God's family. Friendship is the kindness God wants us to show one another.

You bestow on him
blessings forever;
you make him glad with the
joy of your presence.

PSALM 21:6 NRSV

During danger he will
keep me safe in his shelter.
He will hide me in his Holy Tent,
or he will keep me safe on
a high mountain.

PSALM 27:5 NCV

Friends Offer Advice

You will guide me with Your counsel,
And afterward receive me to glory.

PSALM 73:24 NKJV

*T*he Lord works on us through the circumstances of our lives. He has given us friends for inspiration, advice, and correction in our many steps along life's journey.

When you see a friend stumbling or struggling, first pray humbly to the Lord for the wisdom and compassion to reach out and help. Then with the help of the Holy Spirit, offer honest, heartfelt advice for the situation your friend is facing.

It may be a problem at work, with children or a spouse; it may be an emotional or financial difficulty; it may be spiritual drought or confusion about what path to take next in your friend's pilgrimage to God. Large or small, usual or unusual problems plague us because we are human. Allow yourself to be an instrument of peace and love to your friend for the sake of God's love for you.

*R*emain open to God's amazing grace, which will empower us as His instruments to help those who need help. Allow Him to make our hearts responsive and wise in counseling our friends.

Blessed is the man that walketh
not in the counsel of the ungodly,
nor standeth in the way of sinners,
nor sitteth in the seat of the scornful.
But his delight is in the law of the LORD;
and in his law doth he meditate day and night.

PSALM 1:1-2 KJV

Friends Are Faithful

*Nevertheless my lovingkindness
will I not utterly take from him,
nor suffer my faithfulness to fail.*

PSALM 89:33 KJV

A circle of friends, women who had grown up together but had drifted apart, decided to hold a reunion. Everyone in the group was turning fifty that year, and someone had decided that meeting in New York City for a weekend of theater, dining, and shopping would be a grand idea. Elaborate plans were made and mailings were followed by many phone calls. During the planning, bits of news flew back and forth. A few divorces, children graduated from college, career successes and failures, a child lost in a tragic accident, parents' failing health. . . . These were old and dear friends, and they could not wait to be reunited midway in their lives to share memories and news.

At the last minute, one of the women was unable to attend, which disappointed her deeply. The group, however, refused to let her feel forgotten—they called her every day during the weekend to relate each day's events and news.

Let us always hold fast to God's example of steady, unwavering love for our friends.

In him our hearts rejoice,
for we are trusting in his holy name.
Let your unfailing love surround us, LORD,
for our hope is in you alone.

PSALM 33:21-22 NLT

Friends Share Love

For the sake of my relatives and friends
I will say, "Peace be within you."

PSALM 122:8 NRSV

*F*riends have a relationship based on trust, understanding, and shared memories. And each friendship is uniquely defined by the two characters and personalities involved.

Amy and Louise met in a bookstore in the same aisle looking for titles by the same author. They began talking and realized they had read many of the same books and appreciated many of the same qualities about the author: her sense of humor, fine characterization,

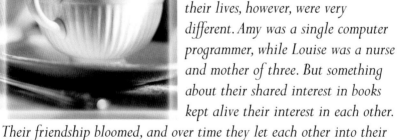

and ability to keep you on the edge of your seat.

After adjourning to the bookstore café for coffee, they discovered that their lives, however, were very different. Amy was a single computer programmer, while Louise was a nurse and mother of three. But something about their shared interest in books kept alive their interest in each other.

Their friendship bloomed, and over time they let each other into their own private worlds, encouraging and supporting each other in their everyday lives.

*G*od delivers to us the people we need and the people who need us. He grants us the ability to recognize and rejoice in these people as His gifts.

May the LORD give you increase more and more,
You and your children.
May you be blessed by the LORD,
Who made heaven and earth.

PSALM 115:14-15 NKJV

The LORD watches over the lives of the innocent,
and their reward will last forever.

PSALM 37:18 NCV

Friends Sympathize

*Give great joy to those
who have stood with me in my defense.*

PSALM 35:27 NLT

Jenny's face appeared suddenly in the kitchen window one June morning. Her eyes were wide and her color was ashen. "What is it?" her mother shrieked, dropping a dish.

"Kelly fell out of the tree!" Jenny yelled. "She can't get up!" The two of them rounded the house at a gallop, Jenny emitting a whine of anxiety. "What if she dies?" she cried in a pitiful voice.

Her mother meanwhile was praying fervently that the injuries weren't serious. She had told the girls previously not to climb too high in trees. But they were at the tomboy stage and enjoyed climbing, like little monkeys.

From a distance, they could see Kelly stretched out at the foot of the maple tree, the family dog standing over her. As they came up to her, breathing hard, Kelly opened her eyes and said, "I'm okay, just had the wind knocked out of me." Jenny helped her up. "Oh, Kelly!" she said. "Thank heavens! You scared me!"

The essence of a friend's sympathy is caring and helping, just as God cares for and helps us. The seeds of sympathy, sowed early, grow deep and strong.

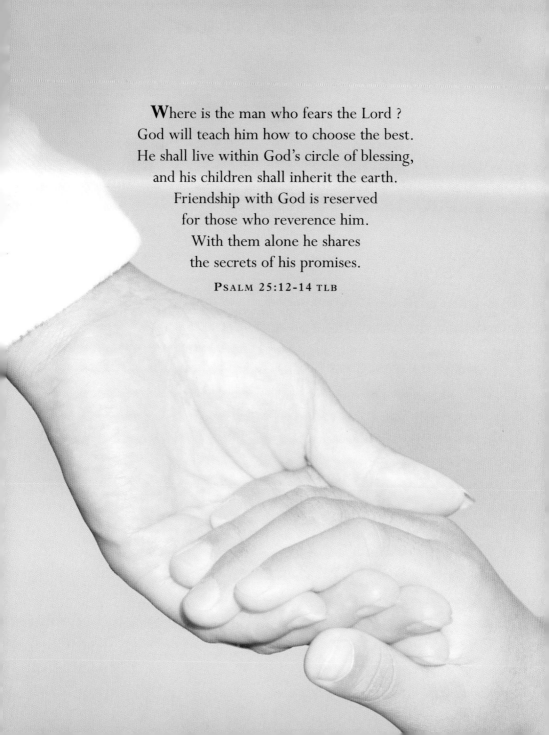

Where is the man who fears the Lord ?
God will teach him how to choose the best.
He shall live within God's circle of blessing,
and his children shall inherit the earth.
Friendship with God is reserved
for those who reverence him.
With them alone he shares
the secrets of his promises.

PSALM 25:12-14 TLB

Friends Understand

I know the LORD is always with me.
I will not be shaken, for he is right beside me.

PSALM 16:8 NLT

A middle-aged woman lived across the street from an elderly man who had recently lost his wife after having been married for more than fifty years. He was not in good health, and his grief was deep and abiding. Over the winter, neighbors looked in on him, visiting and taking him little gifts. When spring came, the man began caring for his late wife's many perennials and roses. The woman across the street saw him in the yard often, tending and cutting flowers. Many times he told her he was getting a bouquet together to take to the cemetery.

By June, the old gentleman began showing up at her front door with flowers. Usually she was in the middle of something, but she knew she had to stop and spend some time with him. She felt his loneliness and suspected she reminded him of his wife at that age.

*L*et us always try to look into the hearts of our friends and meet their needs, even as God knows the deepest needs of our heart and never fails to provide for them.

He led me to a place of safety;
he rescued me because he delights in me.
The LORD rewarded me for doing right;
he compensated me because of my innocence.

PSALM 18:19-20 NLT

Friends Forgive

You are my help.
Because of your protection, I sing.

PSALM 63:7 NCV

*W*hoops! I forgot! Perhaps the most common source of irritation and disappointment between friends has to do with forgetfulness. Forgotten birthdays, anniversaries, lunch dates, promises to do something. . . .And unfortunately, it's so easy to do and such an ordinary human failing, that all of us have been guilty of this sin of omission at some time or another. After all, our lives are busy and we have many responsibilities.

A safety net protects true friendships, though, for they are sustained by unconditional love and trust that each friend is sincere in wanting to do right by the other. Disappointment stings and creates anger, but it passes when friends realize that intentions were good and only the execution was faulty. One of the great comforts of having and being good friends is the knowledge that you are accepting, and accepted—faults and all, just as you are—without having to try to be anyone else.

*G*od will guide us as we try to conform our behavior to His, particularly when we're dealing with forgiveness. All of us make mistakes and need to be forgiving and forgiven.

Yet God was kind.
He kept forgiving their sins
and didn't destroy them.
He often became angry,
but never lost his temper.

PSALM 78:38 CEV

Gracious is the LORD, and righteous;
Yes, our God is merciful.
The LORD preserves the simple;
I was brought low, and He saved me.

PSALM 116:5-6 NKJV

Friends Are Compassionate

Many a time turned he his anger away,
and did not stir up all his wrath.

PSALM 78:38 KJV

"There, but for the grace of God, go I." Compassion is standing in the other person's shoes. Compassion is knowing the same thing could happen to you, or that you could be guilty of the same fault or afraid of the same situation. . . . Compassion is identifying fully with the other person and feeling just as he or she does in trying circumstances, as well as happy times.

Our Lord was full of compassion and is our example. In every instance that Jesus was moved by the sufferings of others, He acted immediately to alleviate their pain.

Being compassionate consistently is not easy. In fact, it hurts. It involves leaving your heart open to all the ups and downs of life that affect others. You become vulnerable, sensitive, and tender. Because the difficulties of others demand a caring response from you, you must become active. You can't just watch from the sidelines; you must reach out and help.

Let us ask God to remove all self-protective hardness from our hearts and send us the grace necessary to be compassionate always.

Jehovah is kind and merciful,
slow to get angry, full of love.
He is good to everyone, and his compassion is
intertwined with everything he does.
All living things shall thank you, Lord,
and your people will bless you.

PSALM 145:8-10 TLB

God, be merciful to me
because you are loving.
Because you are always ready to be merciful,
wipe out all my wrongs.

PSALM 51:1 NCV

They will be so kind
and merciful and good,
that they will be a light
in the dark for others
who do the right thing.

PSALM 112:4 CEV

Friends Stand Fast

I declare that your steadfast love is established forever;
your faithfulness is as firm as the heavens.

PSALM 89:2 NRSV

It's easy to know who your friends are when big trouble hits:
job loss, divorce, serious illness, financial reversal, legal problems. . . .
Acquaintances don't want much to do with sad or desperate situations.
And opportunists don't hang around after you no longer can be of any
use to them.

Bill's business went bust years after he had invested all of his time
and money in it. When he had to file bankruptcy, his wife left with the
kids. He was fifty-nine, and it was hard for him to find a job. It seemed
he had nothing left to lose, including friends. One golfing buddy
remained loyal, as did his bird dog and his former office cleaning lady

who cleaned the studio apartment
he now called home. In this, Bill
found a sobering and inspiring
lesson about friendship. Friends
love you because of who you are,
not what you have. He counted
himself blessed to have three true
friends who had stood the
ultimate test.

Let's pray that we always have the courage to stand by our friends,
and that they, in turn, remain loyal to us.

He that dwelleth in the secret place of the most High
shall abide under the shadow of the Almighty.
I will say of the LORD,
He is my refuge and my fortress:
my God; in him will I trust.

PSALM 91:1-2 KJV

The LORD is my shepherd;
I shall not want.
He makes me to lie down in green pastures;
He leads me beside the still waters.
He restores my soul;
He leads me in the paths of righteousness
For His name's sake.

PSALM 23:1-3 NKJV

Friends Speak the Truth

Justice and judgment are the habitation of thy throne:
mercy and truth shall go before thy face.

PSALM 89:14 KJV

Mary and Lucinda, high-school juniors, went shopping for prom dresses one afternoon. Though shopping was fun, it was serious business picking out just the right ensemble for such an important occasion. The selections were overwhelming in their variety, and it took them hours to narrow the choices down.

Lucinda, who was a perfect size seven, made a choice first. Mary's decision-making was more complicated, because she was more full-figured. But finally Mary fell in love with a dress and asked Lucinda for her approval. Both were tired, and it was late in the day.

Lucinda squirmed as Mary modeled a beautiful midnight blue dress that was formfitting. Mary was wild about it, but it did not flatter her figure. "It's not right," Lucinda said, shaking her head and feeling bad for her friend. "It's too, I don't know, tight or something."

Mary's face fell and she looked hurt. "You mean I'm too fat for it."

"No," Lucinda answered quietly, "it just doesn't make you look as pretty as you are."

No matter how difficult, it is our responsibility to always offer honest, reliable advice to our friends.

A good person speaks with wisdom,
and he says what is fair.
The teachings of his God are in his heart,
so he does not fail to keep them.

PSALM 37:30-31 NCV

God's word is true,
and everything he does is right.
He loves what is right and fair;
the LORD's love fills the earth.

PSALM 33:4-5 NCV

Friends Are Gentle

Unto the upright there ariseth light in the darkness:
he is gracious, and full of compassion.

PSALM 112:4 KJV

*T*he Walkers and Bennetts were weekly tennis doubles partners and had been for more than five years. They had played in a couple of club tournaments together—Bob and Mike pairing off, Betty and Jane teaming up—against other opponents. Their friendship as couples had blossomed and matured over time.

In the last year, Bob Walker's career had stalled and he was having trouble with his boss. Sometimes he would come to their tennis games dragging and down in the mouth. Betty tried to make up for his gloom by being overly cheerful and outgoing. The Bennetts, sensitive to the dynamics of the Walkers' situation, made an extra effort not to step on any toes or push Bob too hard in the match until he had time to loosen up and forget his troubles. Their understanding of the delicate situation and their patience with Bob's moods helped the Walkers through a difficult time.

If we take the time to be gentle with our friends' feelings, God will help us to offer the right comfort and encouragement at the right time.

But as for me, I will sing each morning
about your power and mercy.
For you have been my high tower of refuge,
a place of safety in the day of my distress.
O my Strength, to you I sing my praises;
for you are my high tower of safety,
my God of mercy.

PSALM 59:16-17 TLB

Friends Are Long-Suffering

His heart is fixed, trusting in the LORD.

PSALM 112:7 KJV

Five women had worked together at a publishing company in New York—their first job out of college. As young singles, they became fast friends and did everything together. But when their paths and careers diverged, they made a commitment to stay involved in one another's lives.

As time passed, most married and had children, some left work, most continued in some facet of business. Yet their ties only deepened with each new crisis surmounted, each new milestone in life marked.

When they reached middle age, one of them fell seriously ill, and the prognosis was very bad. The extended chronic illness challenged the women in ways they could not have imagined. They were called to minister to their friend and help each other in handling the sorrow to such a degree that they were strained often to the breaking point. A few found it too difficult and fled for a while, only to return; for despite the heartache of a desperately ill friend, they found the world was far colder outside of that friendship.

When our hearts are fixed on God, we become windows of His constant love to those around us. He gives us an intuitive sense of right behavior, with respect to our friends.

But you, O LORD,
are a God merciful and gracious,
slow to anger and abounding in
steadfast love and faithfulness.

PSALM 86:15 NRSV

But I am like an olive tree,
thriving in the house of God.
I trust in God's unfailing love
Forever and ever.

PSALM 52:8 NLT

Friends Protect Each Other

I have respected your laws,
so keep me safe.

PSALM 119:94 CEV

Everyone has memories of the schoolyard bully and the friends who stood by to protect when he threatened to attack. As we grow older our friends' protection becomes more subtle and complex.

Sarah and Katherine became friends after seeing each other in the

park with their young children a couple of times a week. While the kids played, they exchanged life histories, wishes, hopes, and dreams. While Sarah had a stable, happy marriage, she often picked up clues in conversation that Katherine's home life was less than perfect. One day, a downcast Katherine came to the park with her eyes red and swollen, as if from crying. She offered no explanation for her appearance.

"If you ever need me," Sarah said, as they parted that day, "call me, no matter what time it is, okay?" Katherine looked at Sarah with tears in her eyes and nodded.

"I mean it," Sarah said, squeezing her shoulder.

"I will," Katherine said with a huge sigh of relief. "I will."

As God protects us with His unbounded love, so we are responsible for safeguarding our friends.

You who live in the shelter of the Most High,
who abide in the shadow of the Almighty,
will say to the LORD, "My refuge and my fortress;
my God, in whom I trust."

PSALM 91:1-2 NRSV

Friends Share All

Pour out your unfailing love on those who know you!

PSALM 36:10 TLB

The most valuable commodity we have today is time. Unlike goods and services, extra time in our daily life is in short supply. And friendship requires an investment of time, above all else.

But sharing time with a friend need not be a big issue nor require special preparation. Opportunities exist everywhere for integrating friendships into the overall fabric of our ordinary, daily lives. Indeed, including our friends in the mundane of everyday living draws us nearer and creates family-like ties among us. Friends need to participate in each other's lives, not simply get together for special occasions. Just "hanging out" together—doing things around the house, helping with difficult tasks, or mulling things over—builds intimacy and security among friends. This in turn is relied upon when emergencies or tough times arise, for we know almost intuitively what to do for our friends.

With God's help, we can develop the generosity of spirit to fully become a part of our friends' lives. Then we can give to them in the fullness of our hearts, as He gives of Himself to us.

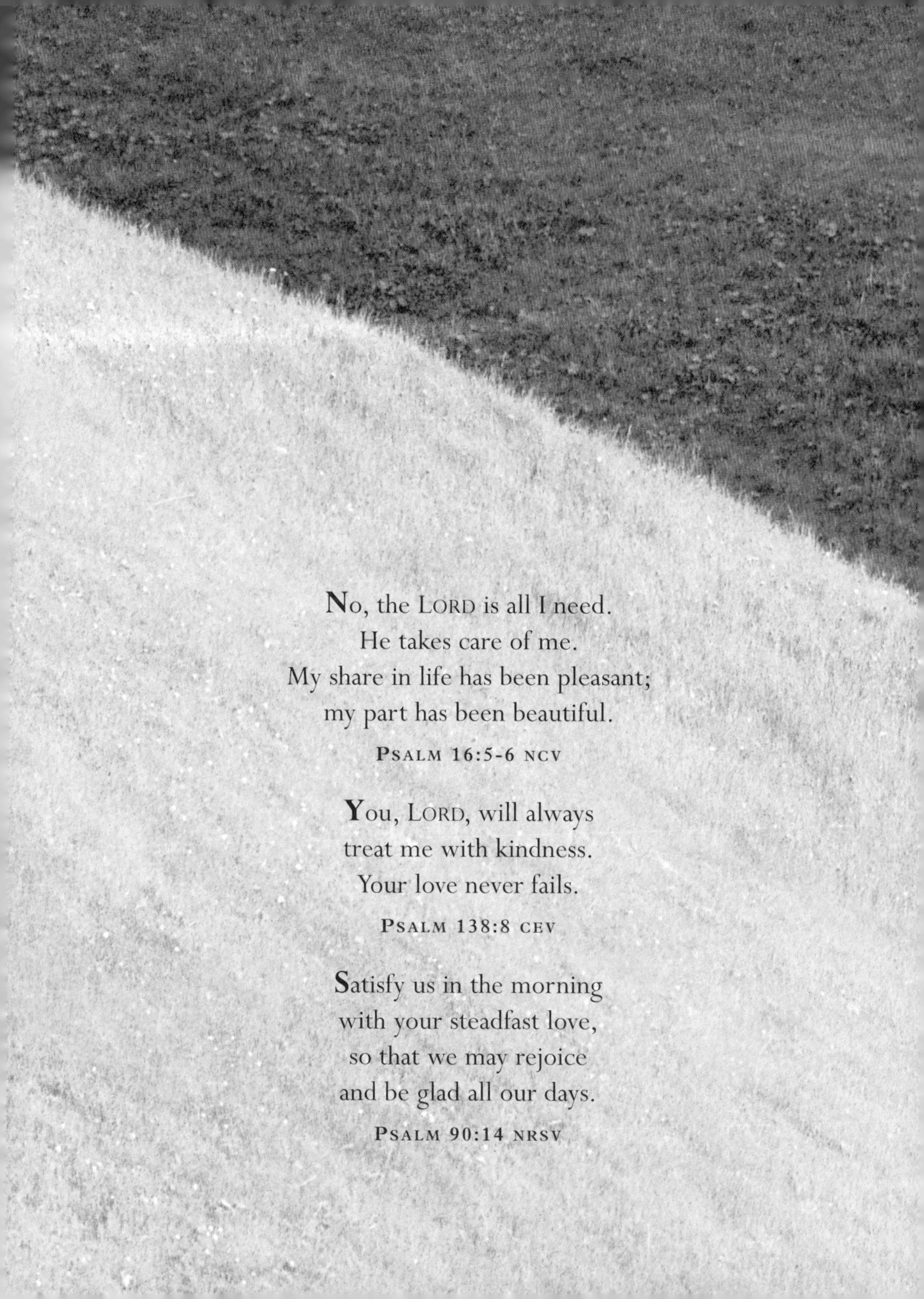

No, the LORD is all I need.
He takes care of me.
My share in life has been pleasant;
my part has been beautiful.

PSALM 16:5-6 NCV

You, LORD, will always
treat me with kindness.
Your love never fails.

PSALM 138:8 CEV

Satisfy us in the morning
with your steadfast love,
so that we may rejoice
and be glad all our days.

PSALM 90:14 NRSV

Friends Enjoy Each Other's Company

Light shines on the godly,
and joy on those who do right.

PSALM 97:11 NLT

The doorbell rang Sunday afternoon as Marty was folding laundry. Monday was already on her mind, with all of the tension of getting the kids to school and herself to the office on time. The work left on her desk Friday afternoon was beginning to haunt her. When she opened the door, her mood softened and brightened. It was Theresa, her friend from down the street.

"You've got to come over and see what I've done with that room!" she cried. "You won't recognize it!" Theresa's face was all smiles.

Marty looked over her shoulder toward the laundry room and the Monday morning gaining on her. "Gee . . ." she said, hesitating.

Theresa insisted, pulling her arm. "It'll only take a minute!"

Marty's spirits lifted as she walked down the front steps. She knew Theresa had been pondering for weeks what color to paint the spare bedroom. Marty couldn't wait to share in her pleasure and surprise.

The visitation of a good friend is like a breath from heaven. Her companionship is a blessing from God that bolsters and comforts us.

Examine and see how good the LORD is.
Happy is the person who trusts him.

PSALM 34:8 NCV

The LORD God is famous
for his wonderful deeds,
and he is kind and merciful.

PSALM 111:4 CEV

I will thank you, LORD, with all my heart;
I will tell of all the marvelous things you have done.
I will be filled with joy because of you.
I will sing praises to your name, O Most High.

PSALM 9:1-2 NLT

Friends Work Side by Side

The godly people in the land are my true heroes!
I take pleasure in them!

PSALM 16:3 NLT

"I need your help," Jessica said to Shelly, pointing to the petition she was holding. "This needs five hundred signatures by next Saturday if it's going to do any good."

Jess had been explaining to Shelly, her next-door neighbor and friend, that the petition— one of twenty like it—concerned the proposed sale of the local hospital to a large for-profit healthcare corporation. She was against it for several reasons, including the fact that hundreds of people would lose their jobs, the nurse-patient ratio would decline drastically, and community volunteer involvement would deteriorate.

Shelly wasn't familiar with the cause, but she was moved by Jess's fervor. Glancing at the last page of the document, she noted that fewer than a hundred people had signed it thus far. This was going to be an uphill battle for Jess.

"Okay, Jess," Shelly said. "Let me look it over tonight. It seems pretty important." Shelly knew that she needed to take her friend seriously and lend a hand with her concerns.

Some of the most important work we will ever do is alongside our friends, supporting their beliefs and convictions.

Thou wilt shew me the path of life:
in thy presence is fulness of joy;
at thy right hand there are pleasures for evermore.

PSALM 16:11 KJV

But all who humble themselves
before the Lord
shall be given every blessing,
and shall have wonderful peace.

PSALM 37:11 TLB

Friends Make Sacrifices

He has delivered me from every trouble,
and my eye has looked in triumph on my enemies.

*J*erry and Janet hadn't had a weekend to themselves in months. Jerry had been traveling on business, and Janet, a medical doctor, had been on weekend rotations at the emergency room. Though they spoke over the phone, they still felt the distance between them and longed for some quiet time at home relaxing together.

Friday night as they were sitting in front of the TV with their arms linked, they received a frantic phone call. It was Allen and Barb, who were moving that weekend.

"I hate to ask this," Barb said, her voice full of regret, "but we've had a problem with the movers. . . ."

Janet looked across the room at her weary husband. "And you need help, right?" she asked. She put her hand over the receiver and explained to Jerry. They recalled their own difficulties with moving.

"Let's do it," Jerry said, finally.

"You bet," Janet replied.

*T*he demands that love places upon the heart are rarely convenient or moderate. But as God is always there for us, we must be available to our friends when they need us.

I will give thanks to the LORD with my whole heart,
in the company of the upright, in the congregation.
Great are the works of the LORD,
studied by all who delight in them.
Full of honor and majesty is his work,
and his righteousness endures forever.

PSALM 111:1-3 NRSV

Friends Pray Together

In the day when I cried out, You answered me,
And made me bold with strength in my soul.

PSALM 138:3 NKJV

Joan, Allie, and Betsy have an active and fruitful prayer group. Every week they exchange prayer requests and spend a half-hour a day praying for the items on the list. Their prayer requests are specific and timely, relating to what is really going on in their lives. They also include big requests, such as world peace, the salvation of souls, and a solution to world hunger.

They have prayed like this for years, ever since Allie's father fell seriously ill and was in intensive care. During his illness they met over the phone three times a day in a conference call, asking God to make him well. Allie's father recovered, and the three friends developed a deepened spirituality and prayer life. Their prayers have continued to be answered in ways they could not have dreamed possible. They give credit to God for the security, joy, and abundance they have found in their lives.

Let us pray that our friends, and everyone's friends, discover the joy and comfort of praying for and with each other.

Accept my prayer as incense offered to you,
and my upraised hands as an evening offering.

PSALM 141:2 NLT

What can I offer the LORD
for all he has done for me?
I will lift up a cup symbolizing his salvation;
I will praise the LORD's name for saving me.

PSALM 116:12-13 NLT

Friends Receive Special Blessings from God

My life is an example to many,
because you have been my strength and protection.

PSALM 71:7 NLT

*F*riendship develops and grows and prospers over time. It requires space and grace. Like a huge tree, it needs to root deeply and spread its branches. With each obstacle overcome, each crisis survived, and many ordinary days in between, it becomes stronger and more valuable, in exactly the same way that our relationship with the Lord deepens and flourishes as we repeatedly seek His company and help.

As we know, the Lord works through His people. He sends us friends to aid and comfort us. When we recognize this and give thanks and stick with our friends, abundant blessings flow to us, both individually and in the friendship relationship.

God honors friendships with special blessings and strength. The lives of our friends reflect the confidence and grace the Lord bestows, and they become shining examples to others.

*L*et us allow God to guide us and teach us to be loyal and giving friends so that we may be instruments of His glory and grace in the world.

The LORD will give strength to His people;
The LORD will bless His people with peace.

PSALM 29:11 NKJV

But I, through the abundance of your steadfast love,
will enter your house,
I will bow down toward your holy temple
in awe of you.

PSALM 5:7 NRSV

Friends Are United

Gail and Linda were neighbors who both had teenage daughters attending the same high school. Although the girls had different personalities, they were good friends and did just about everything together. Gail's daughter, Susie, was an extrovert and always full of energy; while Linda's daughter, Marie, was relatively shy and reserved. They were a good pair, for they tempered each other's excesses and had complementary traits.

One evening Marie went to her mother with troubling news. Someone had been spreading reputation-wrecking rumors around school about Susie's behavior with boys and drugs. Marie knew these stories were untrue, but she feared for Susie, who was terribly upset about them.

All four of the friends—both mothers and both daughters—went to see the guidance counselor at school the next day. They confronted the problem as a group and received immediate results from the school authorities, thus ending the spread of all damaging rumors.

God watches over our friends and protects them; He gives us the courage to stand by them when they need us and the wisdom to do what is right.

I have set the LORD always before me:
because he is at my right hand,
I shall not be moved.
Therefore my heart is glad,
and my glory rejoiceth:
my flesh also shall rest in hope.

PSALM 16:8-9 KJV

Friends Are Generous

You give your guests a feast in your house,
and you serve a tasty drink that flows like a river.

PSALM 36:8 CEV

Three sorority sisters shared everything from hair dryers and clothes to food, money, cars, and textbooks. When they graduated, they kept in touch and got together each summer at a beach cottage. There, they spent a week in the sun catching up on the year's news, reading, reminiscing, and laying plans for the great things they were going to do in life. Always they exchanged information, contacts, and advice—anything one had that another needed.

It was a special time in the year to which they always looked forward—reuniting with best friends, giving of themselves to maintain the friendship, and helping each other individually. In fact, the three women, now middle-aged with grown children, still continue the tradition. For them, the time spent together is one of the big highlights of their year and an important factor in their lives.

God can teach us to extend ourselves for our friends and give to them abundantly. Through God's abundant generosity, we learn the joy of giving and the blessings derived from it.

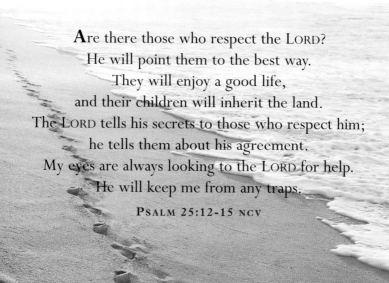

Are there those who respect the LORD?
He will point them to the best way.
They will enjoy a good life,
and their children will inherit the land.
The LORD tells his secrets to those who respect him;
he tells them about his agreement.
My eyes are always looking to the LORD for help.
He will keep me from any traps.

PSALM 25:12-15 NCV

Friends Bring Out the Best

Delight thyself also in the LORD;
and he shall give thee the desires of thine heart.

PSALM 37:4 KJV

There are many tests of friendship. But perhaps the ultimate test lies in how effective the relationship is in bringing each friend closer to God. Worldly achievements and success usually attach themselves to believers; however, that is not the point of our lives. The "best" that we can be truly means to completely conform our lives to God and, thereby, find true happiness and peace.

We must make deepened spirituality the measure of the quality of our friendships. Are we encouraging spiritual growth, prayer, moral and ethical development, and participation in a community of believers? Do we avoid putting our friends in the way of temptations? Do we forbear from contributing to behavior that is dangerous to the health of their souls? Do we offer consistent, selfless encouragement and advice directed to the well-being and growth of our friends' spiritual lives?

We must strive to achieve the grace necessary to bring out the best in our friends and to do all we can to bring them ever closer to God.

The godly shall be firmly planted in the land,
and live there forever.
The godly man is a good counselor
because he is just and fair
and knows right from wrong.

PSALM 37:29-31 TLB

Friends Inspire
Each Other

Bless the LORD, O my soul.

PSALM 104:1 KJV

"*Look at you! Look at what you've done!*"*Heidi yelled across the fairway. Her golfing partner, Linda, had effortlessly birdied the first hole; this, after confessing to Heidi before they teed off that she was convinced her golf game had gone from bad to worse. She was even thinking of giving it up altogether. This statement had really concerned Heidi, because their weekly game was the only regular time they were able to spend together.*

"That's a really tough hole, kiddo," Heidi said as she putted out two over par. "I'm proud of you. Look how you can play when you stop trying so hard!" Linda smiled ruefully. "Maybe I've turned the corner," she said. Linda was thinking, though, about what a great gal Heidi really was. She never stopped encouraging her, never teased too hard when she flubbed a shot . . . how much she enjoyed being with her.

When we search for the right words and tone of voice, we can be a source of hope and inspiration to our friends in matters both great and small.

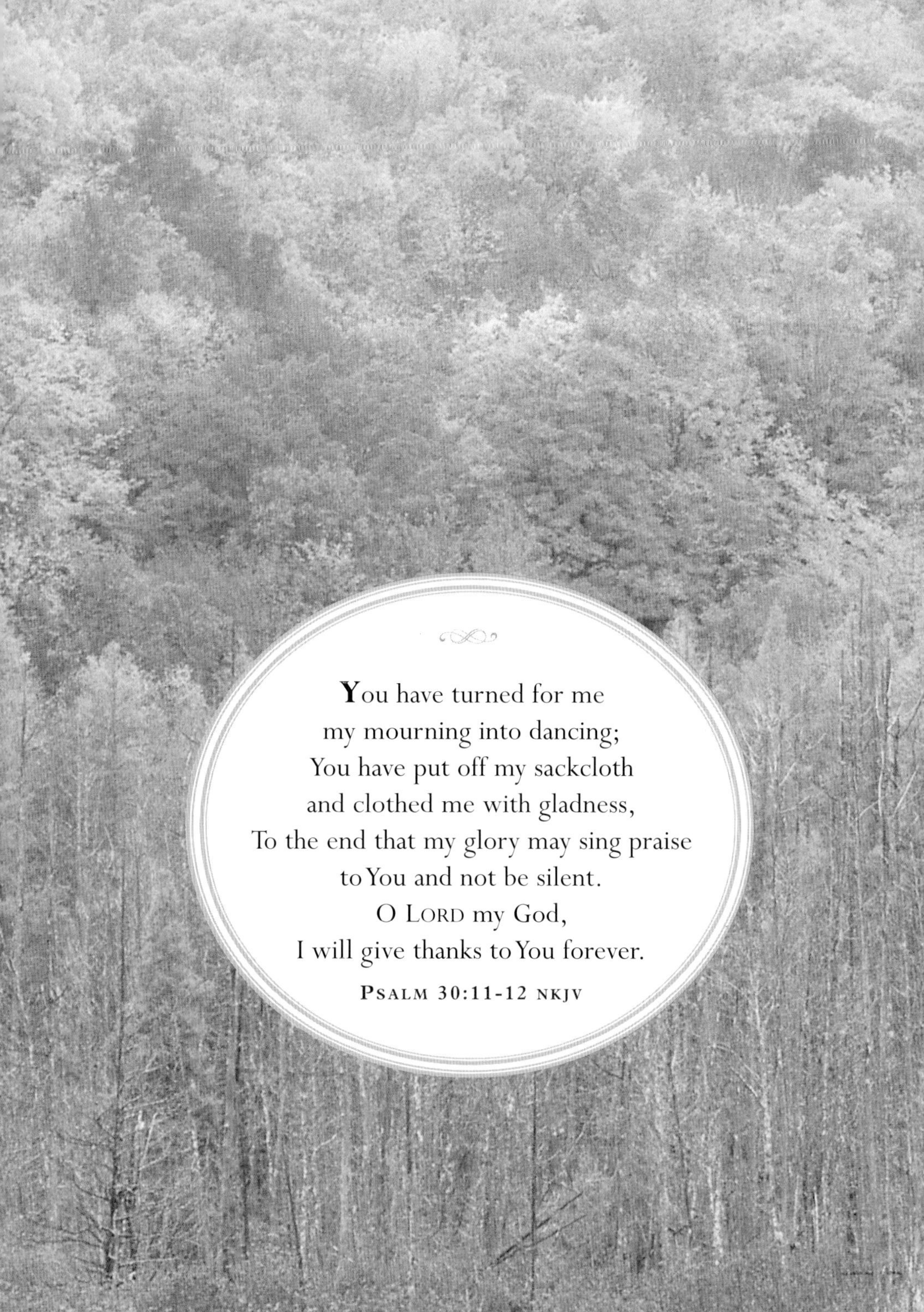

You have turned for me
my mourning into dancing;
You have put off my sackcloth
and clothed me with gladness,
To the end that my glory may sing praise
to You and not be silent.
O Lord my God,
I will give thanks to You forever.

PSALM 30:11-12 NKJV

Friends Encourage
Each Other

*Everyone finds shelter
in the shadow of your wings.*

PSALM 36:7 CEV

*K*aren had always wanted to be an artist. More than anything else, she loved to paint and draw. But financial constraints kept her from pursuing her dream with all of her time and energy. To contribute to the family income, she worked as an x-ray technician at a local hospital. Weekends, though, she pursued her artwork. Finally, after years, she had enough work to take to an art show.

Her friend Deborah, a nurse, had watched and nurtured Karen's

artistic pursuits—always asking about what she was working on, analyzing it, and praising it. She knew the importance of following your dreams and making use of the talents God has given you. Deborah was right there, pitching in, when the time came for Karen to go to the art show. She helped her set up and stayed with her as the general public viewed her work for the first time. Her encouragement to Karen was immeasurable.

*W*e must look into the hearts of our friends, discern what makes them who they are, and nurture their uniqueness so they can flower as the Lord intends.

Because of my friends
and my relatives,
I will pray for peace.
And because of the house
of the LORD our God,
I will work for your good.

PSALM 122:8-9 CEV

LORD, show your love to us
as we put our hope in you.

PSALM 33:22 NCV

Friends Dream Together

Let heaven and earth praise Him,
The seas and everything that moves in them.

PSALM 69:34 NKJV

*C*arpooling to and from work gave Sara, Lynn, and Jeanie
plenty of time over the year to get to know one another. Creeping
along in rush-hour traffic, they developed a friendship and knowledge
of one another's family and interests. They drew close; for they
genuinely liked each other and came to share their wishes, hopes,
and dreams.

Sara, more than anything else, hoped her
young son would continue with his piano
lessons and practice, because he showed signs
of being a child prodigy. Lynn and her
husband were planning their dream home and
hoped to begin construction within a year.
Jeanie wanted to finish her college degree and
hoped to find the time and money to do just
that—although the way things stood now, she
couldn't see how that could be accomplished.

The more they opened up to one another, the more their friendship
grew. They came to share their individual aspirations, until they truly
had invested themselves in the others' dreams. They began to pray for
each other that these dreams would become a reality; and as they did,
their confidence grew and real progress was made.

*A*n important part of friendship is becoming vulnerable and open
enough to participate in the dreams of others.

I heard God say two things:
"I am powerful,
and I am very kind."
The Lord rewards each of us
according to what we do.

PSALM 62:11-12 CEV

Be still in the presence of the LORD,
and wait patiently for him to act.

PSALM 37:7 NLT

God Blesses the Bonds
of Friendship

*The godly man is a good counselor
because he is just and fair and knows right from wrong.*

PSALM 37:30-31 TLB

Two women who had been friends for years decided to open a catering business together. They had given the idea and their business plan a great deal of thought and had reviewed it with accountants and outside advisors. The feedback they had gotten was unanimously positive; most said they had rarely seen a plan so thoroughly thought out, down to the last details involving marketing and publicity.

Both women were hard workers, creative and energetic, and they had "been around the block before," so they weren't naive about the difficulties and obstacles they would encounter at start-up. They prayerfully sought guidance from God in their decision, as well as help from Him in building the business.

One of the things that really set the new business apart from other "wannabes" was the pair's knowledge, understanding, and confidence in each other. They had been through tough times together before. They knew each other so well, and trusted each other and God so implicitly, that they made a winning team.

When we seek God's guidance with our friendships, He will never let us down, but will strengthen and bless them abundantly.

Commit everything you do to the LORD.
Trust him, and he will help you.
He will make your innocence as clear as the dawn,
and the justice of your cause will shine like the noonday sun.

PSALM 37:5-6 NLT

Friends Rest in Each Other's Strength

The good man does not escape all troubles—
he has them too.
But the Lord helps him in each and every one.

PSALM 34:19 TLB

*C*hristina was having "one of those days." Everything was running about an hour late: her dentist appointment, her trip to the grocery store. The traffic was awful . . . then, as she was speeding along the interstate en route to Happy Camper Childcare to pick up little Travis, she heard a horrible bang! And her car lurched to the right, nearly careening over the shoulder of the roadbed into a ditch. When it finally came to a stop and she had stopped shaking, she realized she had had a blowout.

Now what?! The ice cream was melting, the chicken was defrosting, the Novocain was wearing off, her jaw hurt . . . and worst of all, Happy Camper Childcare would close in fifteen minutes and Travis would be out on the street!

Then suddenly a little corner of peace entered her heart. She fumbled for her cell phone and punched in a number she had on direct dial.

"Lisa?" she gasped when her friend answered. "Thank God you're home! You won't believe what happened. . . ."

*O*ur friends are God's angels sent to us to keep us safe. Let us praise Him and thank Him for the wonderful gift of friendship.

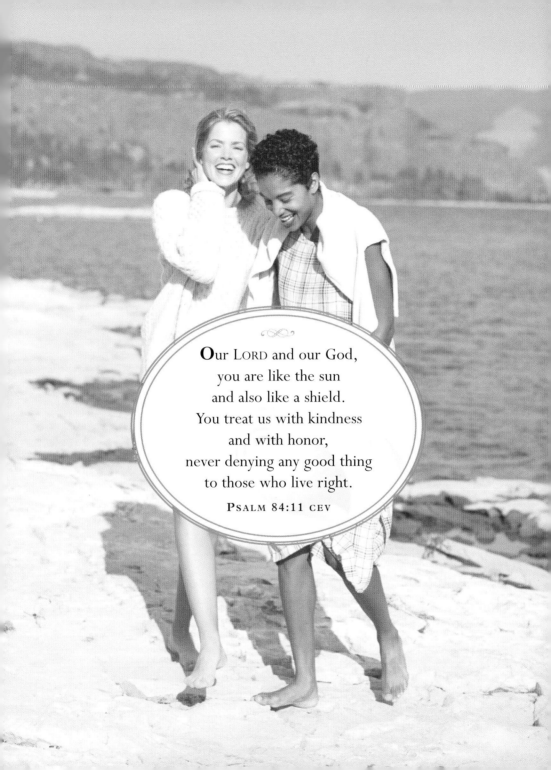

Our LORD and our God,
you are like the sun
and also like a shield.
You treat us with kindness
and with honor,
never denying any good thing
to those who live right.

PSALM 84:11 CEV

Friends Correct Each Other

I will advise you and watch your progress.

*M*artha listened and felt her own heart sinking as Abby's voice rose with enthusiasm. Abby was describing the dining room suite she had run across at a furniture store. It was just what she had been looking for, and it was, best of all, on sale.

"And you know better than anyone, Martha," she said, "how long I've been trying to find a southwest style around here where there are nothing but nineteenth-century reproductions!"

"Yes, but—" Martha murmured, before being interrupted.

"I'd be crazy to pass this up. The store will do its own financing, and I can just afford the payment." Abby paused and sighed.

"I thought you'd made it a priority, though, to pay off your credit cards, Abby," Martha finally was able to say. She tensed, knowing this was absolutely not what her friend wanted to hear at this particular moment. But she had to say it. Both had agreed just last week that Abby was getting in over her head and needed to curb her spending.

---

*G*od uses us to guide and correct our friends as needed. If we are attentive to Him, He will put the right words in our mouths and the right spirit in our hearts so that we may do this gently.

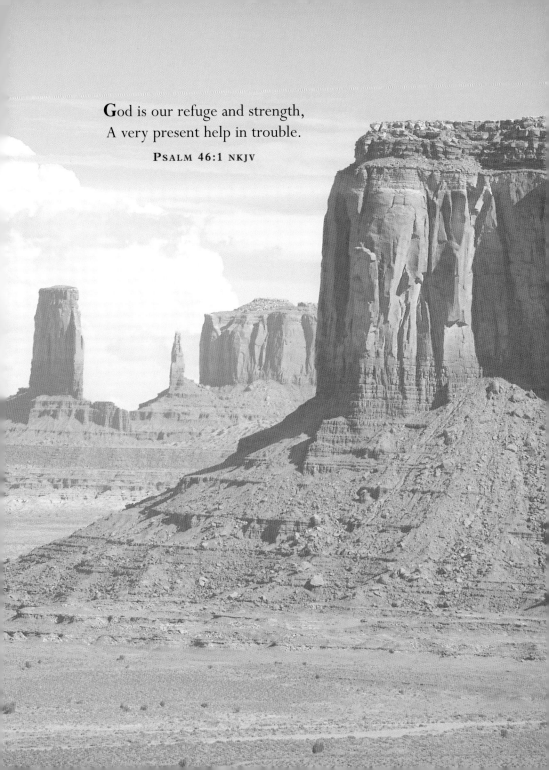

God is our refuge and strength,
A very present help in trouble.

PSALM 46:1 NKJV

Friends Look Out
for Each Other

*For the eyes of the Lord are intently watching
all who live good lives.*

PSALM 34:15 TLB

Stephanie had been thinking about it all Saturday morning
and finally picked up the phone. Betsy answered after three rings.

"You've been on my mind all morning, Bets. I even had a dream
about you last night," Stephanie said.

Betsy laughed. "That's funny," she said. "I've been down in the
dumps the last couple of days. I'm having trouble at work again."

Steph had a sudden inspiration. "Let's go over the classified ads
together this Sunday, Bets. I'm sure if we put our heads together, we
could come up with some alternatives for you."

Bets groaned.

"No, it'll be fun! You've got to start somewhere."

"You're right, Steph. Thanks for pushing me to get going on it."

When we care deeply for our friends, we become attuned to their
well-being and many times intuitively know when something is wrong.
We become extensions of God's love and grace for them in the world.

Every morning tell him,
"Thank you for your kindness,"
and every evening rejoice
in all his faithfulness.

PSALM 92:2 TLB

Lord, when doubts fill my mind,
when my heart is in turmoil,
quiet me and give me
renewed hope and cheer.

PSALM 94:19 TLB

Friends Do Not Cause Each Other to Stumble

Show me Your ways, O LORD;
Teach me your paths.

PSALM 25:4 NKJV

*K*atie's doctor laid down the law: Her blood pressure and cholesterol were dangerously high, and she had to lose thirty pounds. He gave her a diet to follow and set her up for weekly weigh-ins.

Cora, her friend, had been worried about Katie's health and was glad that someone had finally gotten through to her, but she knew the diet was not going to be easy for Katie. She had a terrible sweet tooth, and when stressed or unhappy she would automatically reach for the candy and milkshakes.

Cora realized she was going to have to change her own behavior around Katie to help her. No more stops at the ice-cream parlor on the way to the mall, no more brownies or strawberry shortcake for dessert when they dined at her house. She would have to provide lots of comfort and support, and praise Katie at every appropriate opportunity.

*S*acrifice is often required of friends for the good of the other. And it is particularly important to support our friends in their battles against human weaknesses.

I will try to walk a blameless path,
but how I need your help,
especially in my own home,
where I long to act as I should.

PSALM 101:2 TLB

Friends Steady Each Other

Yes, Lord, let your constant love surround us,
for our hopes are in you alone.

PSALM 33:22 TLB

*E*mily was terrified of the presentation she had to give at work. She practiced deep breathing and memorized her talk in the hopes that these tactics would see her through. Even so, every time she pictured herself standing before the group, she felt faint and her lips and fingernails turned blue.

Her friend Cherise knew all about fears and tried to think of things that would alleviate her nervousness. Emily knew her material and was ready for any questions the audience might have. It wasn't a matter of preparation. The issue was one of confidence.

Cherise suggested they pray and ask God to take care of Emily's presentation delivery. They prayed together over the phone every night for a week, asking specifically for help with the questions. Emily really believed God would intervene, but she wasn't sure she could hold up her end of the bargain. Then, the morning before her speech, Cherise gave her something to hang on to during the presentation. When Emily was called to the podium she went with her papers in one hand and a small cross in the other. She was dazzling.

*W*e can give our concerns about our friends to God, and ask Him to help us reach out in the best way when they need us.

LORD, I trust in you;
let me never be disgraced.
Save me because you do what is right.

PSALM 31:1 NCV

The LORD also will be a refuge for the oppressed,
A refuge in times of trouble.
And those who know Your name
will put their trust in You;
For You, LORD, have not forsaken
those who seek You.

PSALM 9:9-10 NKJV

Friends Celebrate Each Other's Victories

He shall live within God's circle of blessing,
and his children shall inherit the earth.

PSALM 25:13 TLB

Diane, a single mother, was a soccer mom but not an ordinary one. Her daughter, Lynn, had played soccer since she was a tiny little girl and now was a star on her high-school team.

Now Lynn had a chance at a full scholarship at a great university. Diane was elated, because college tuition would have been a huge burden for her.

Her friends got wind of this and came out in full force for each game to cheer Lynn on and to support Diane. They brought pom-poms, horns, kazoos, and lawn chairs; and they lined up as a group on the sidelines, yelling at the top of their lungs for Lynn and her team.

Lynn won the scholarship, to no one's real surprise, and went on to become an athlete and scholar in college.

God wants His children to be happy and to prosper, to have a cause to celebrate. He gives us friends to be with us in our moments of triumph and joy.

It is wonderful to be grateful
and to sing your praises,
LORD, Most High!
It is wonderful each morning
to tell about your love
and at night to announce
how faithful you are.

PSALM 92:1-2 CEV

Friends Bear Each Other Up

The LORD is the strength of my life;
Of whom shall I be afraid?

PSALM 27:1 NKJV

The waiting room was so quiet the fluorescent lights could be heard humming. Tears streaked John and Megan's faces. Ted and Ashley sat across from them, tense with sympathy.

"Why is it taking so long?" Megan sighed, wiping her nose.

"It's only been twenty minutes since the doctor was here," Ashley said, reaching out for Megan's hand. "Just keep praying. Let God handle it."

"But he's so small . . ." Megan began. Her husband put his arm around her.

John and Megan's son, Matt, had cystic fibrosis, and his life lurched from crisis to crisis. Despite the fine treatment he received, there were still scary episodes when his illness flared up.

Ted and Ashley knew that just their presence in the waiting room was critically important for their neighbors. In standing by their sides, they were offering the hope and consolation God wants us to have in the dark hours of our lives.

When moments arrive where we must be strong and comforting, nothing stands out more than simply "being there" for our friends.

Satisfy us in the morning with your unfailing love,
so we may sing for joy to the end of our lives.
Give us gladness in proportion to our former misery!
Replace the evil years with good.
Let us see your miracles again;
let our children see your glory at work.

PSALM 90:14-16 NLT

Friends Are Reliable

Who is as mighty as you, O LORD?
Your faithfulness surrounds you.

PSALM 89:8 NRSV

"Don't worry. I'll be there," Erin said as Kathy waved and walked away. Erin looked down at Billy, Kathy's four-year-old, to see if he was going to cry. Kathy had left him with her so she could shop unencumbered for his birthday presents. They were to meet in the mall's food court in one hour.

Billy, Erin decided, was doing just fine. If she could only keep him quiet and entertained for a while, his mother would be back before he knew she was gone. Kathy smiled to herself and glanced at Billy again. His face was beet red now, and tears sprouted from his eyes. . . .

Erin quickly took Billy to get a frozen yogurt and then over to a toy store where they spent a pleasant hour in the action-figure department. Later, Kathy returned, burdened with packages, to the food court. There she found a smiling duo waiting for her, absorbed with a coloring book.

"He was a perfect angel," Erin said.

Good friends make God their guide for their behavior. His unswerving loyalty and constant concern for His creation set the standard for the relationship.

The LORD says, "I will rescue those who love me.
I will protect those who trust in my name.
When they call on me, I will answer;
I will be with them in trouble.
I will rescue them and honor them.
I will satisfy them with a long life
and give them my salvation."

PSALM 91:14-16 NLT

Only God gives inward peace,
and I depend on him.
God alone is the mighty rock
that keeps me safe,
and he is the fortress
where I feel secure.

PSALM 62:5-6 CEV

Friends Provide Reality Checks

For You are my rock and my fortress;
Therefore, for Your name's sake,
Lead me and guide me.

"This is nuts", Jackie said to herself as Heather described what she planned to do with her savings and 401(k) plan: Put all the money into an online brokerage for day-trading. She was sure that with the momentum the market had, she couldn't fail.

"Do you really think that is a good idea, Heather?" Jackie asked. "That's all of your retirement, isn't it?"

"Can't miss," Heather said, firmly.

"Promise me one thing," Jackie said. "Promise me you'll wait until you've talked to your accountant."

Heather looked puzzled. "I get the impression you don't think this is the smartest thing I've ever come up with," she said.

"You're right!" Jackie said. "For Pete's sake, Heather, think of the risk. Think of little Mary and Joey. Do you want them to have to take care of you when you're elderly?"

Miffed, Heather said, "Okay! I'll talk to my accountant!"

It's never easy taking the wind out of our loved ones' sails, but when we see them pursuing a dangerous path, it's a responsibility, God says, we cannot shirk.

Our God comes, and he will not be silent.
A fire burns in front of him,
and a powerful storm surrounds him.

PSALM 50:3 NCV

His name shall endure forever;
His name shall continue as long as the sun.
And men shall be blessed in Him;
All nations shall call Him blessed.

PSALM 72:17 NKJV

Friends Endure
Through Time

You have been with me from birth;
from my mother's womb you have cared for me.

PSALM 71:6 NLT

*O*ld friend is a phrase that evokes warmth and comfort, and for good reason. Our best friends, our most solid and beloved friends, are those who have stood the test of time. They have forgiven our oversights, silliness, every kind of foolishness, petty offenses, and large mistakes. They have seen us at our best, as well as our worst. They know our strengths and our weaknesses.

Old friends have a bedrock of shared memories that nothing can take away. They have developed a shorthand for communication because they know each other so well. They understand each other so well that "getting along" is not an issue. Instead, each other's company is a solace and source of quiet joy. They can happily spend an afternoon together without saying a word.

The ups and downs of life, the many trials of true friendship, have been weathered and overcome. Old friends flourish in the light they create for each other, and they may call themselves blessed.

*W*e can pray that we receive the grace for friendship that endures, for it is one of God's greatest gifts and a gift that will bring us closer to Him.

They will be so kind
and merciful and good,
that they will be a light
in the dark for others
who do the right thing.
Life will go well for those
who freely lend and are honest in business.
They won't ever be troubled,
and the kind things they do
will never be forgotten.

PSALM 112:4-6 CEV

I will keep a protective eye on the godly,
so they may dwell with me in safety.
Only those who are above reproach
will be allowed to serve me.

PSALM 101:6 NLT

Friends Are Accepting

For His anger is but for a moment,
His favor is for life.

PSALM 30:5 NKJV

If Amy was on time for anything, you can be sure it was an accident. She was one of those people who tried to cram as much activity into any given hour in the day as was humanly possible. The result: She was always twenty or thirty minutes late, sometimes more.

Sharon and Amy had been friends for years, but Amy's habitual

tardiness almost nipped the friendship in the bud. For Sharon, promptness was a matter of honor and principle. Being late was irresponsible and inconsiderate. It meant that the tardy person thought so little of another's time that she refused to keep to a schedule.

Finally, after Amy missed a plane and was fired from a job because of her tardiness, Sharon realized Amy had a problem. Sharon softened and wanted to help. And try to help she did . . . but with very modest improvement on Amy's part. Yet Amy was such a wonderful caring person in every other way, Sharon at last conceded being late was just part of being Amy. She resolved to love her just the way she was.

No one is perfect, let us remember, including ourselves. Accepting and forgiving our friends' faults is one of the demands of friendship, just as the Lord accepts and forgives us for our own shortcomings.

Examine me, O LORD, and prove me;
Try my mind and my heart.
For Your lovingkindness is before my eyes,
And I have walked in Your truth.

PSALM 26:2-3 NKJV

Friends Provide Hugs

The LORD is close to the brokenhearted,
and he saves those whose spirits have been crushed.
PSALM 34:18 NCV

"You look like you need a hug," Nancy said, as her friend walked into the room. "What's the matter?"

"I don't know. I just don't have much energy," Nita said. Her expression was blank, and her shoulders slumped a little.

Nancy went up to her and put her arm around her. "Are you getting enough sleep, kiddo?"

Tears sprang to Nita's eyes. "I'm not getting enough of anything!" she whispered under her breath.

"You've been working too hard, and with the kids and all, it's just too much. You need a little break." Nancy squeezed her shoulder.

Tears ran down Nita's cheeks. "I looked at the trash stacked up in the garage, and it was the last straw. Those big, black plastic bags. . . ." She covered her face.

"I've got an idea," Nancy said. "You and Ted take the weekend off, do something fun. Let me take care of the kids and clean your house. It's just what you need."

Nita looked at Nancy through her fingers. "I couldn't do that. . . ."

"You could and you will!" Nancy said, giving her a big hug.

Friends serve and minister to one another's needs, generously and selflessly, in matters great and small.

You are kind, LORD,
so good and merciful.
You protect ordinary people,
and when I was helpless,
you saved me
and treated me so kindly
that I don't need
to worry anymore.

PSALM 116:5-7 CEV

Friends Are There When the World Abandons Us

I asked the LORD for help, and he answered me.
He saved me from all that I feared.

PSALM 34:4 NCV

*A*manda's life had been in a downward spiral for some time. Her increasingly erratic and rash behavior had resulted in bounced checks, heavy debts, speeding tickets, and the loss of her driver's license and had put her teaching job on the line. Her condo was a mess, and the plumbing in one bathroom was backed up. Almost everyone thought irresponsible willfulness on her part was to blame. Everyone, that is, but her old college friend Ruth. Ruth remembered the old Amanda, the "real" Amanda. Ruth convinced her to see a doctor to talk over the all the "bad luck" (as Ruth called it) that she was having. The doctor discovered that a sizable brain tumor was causing her strange behavior, and immediately scheduled surgery. Fortunately, the operation was successful and, over a period of time, Amanda regained her health and was able to pick up the pieces to rebuild her life.

*V*ery simply, God will never forsake us and we must never forsake our friends. The love of friendship, as an extension of God's love for the world, is unconditional and unchanging.

You, LORD, have saved
my life from death,
my eyes from tears,
my feet from stumbling.
Now I will walk at your side
in this land of the living.
I was faithful to you
when I was suffering,
though in my confusion I said,
"I can't trust anyone!"

PSALM 116:8-11 CEV

Friends Minister to Each Other's Wounds

Depend on the LORD;
trust him, and he will take care of you.

PSALM 37:5 NCV

Lauren, who was slated to be a June bride, was shocked and crushed when her fiancé backed out of the engagement in the middle of May. Invitations had gone out, the church had been reserved, the bridesmaids had ordered their dresses. Lauren was numb with embarrassment and disappointment. Nothing in her fiancé's previous behavior had given any clue that something like this might happen.

She wanted to crawl into a hole and die. All her plans for the future had imploded, and she no longer knew who she was nor what she should be doing.

Ivy, who was to have been her maid of honor, suggested they take a trip together using the time Lauren had set aside for the honeymoon. Ivy would take an emergency leave from work; and they would drive west, across the country, to the Grand Canyon, Colorado, and California. As the miles passed, Lauren would decompress and heal in the company of her good friend. Maybe they would even start laying plans for a new, improved future for Lauren.

When bad things happen to our friends, we must step up without hesitation, as God does for us, and soothe and support them.

They that sow in tears
shall reap in joy.
He that goeth forth and weepeth,
bearing precious seed,
shall doubtless come again with rejoicing,
bringing his sheaves with him.

PSALM 126:5-6 KJV

Steadfast love and faithfulness will meet;
righteousness and peace will kiss each other.
Faithfulness will spring up from the ground,
and righteousness will look down from the sky.

PSALM 85:10-11 NRSV

Friends Can Keep Secrets

*Trust the L*ORD *and do good.*
Live in the land and feed on truth.

PSALM 37:3 NCV

*K*eeping a secret can be very difficult. There's something about a secret that puts pressure on you, that makes you feel like you'll explode if you can't share the burden of it.

Secrets come in many flavors and varieties. Happy surprises, great  news . . . shameful or sad . . . silly and funny . . . . The point being, with a secret, information must be contained until the proper time arrives when it can be disclosed. And for some secrets (of the bad variety) that means the Second Coming.

There's a maxim that says if you want to keep a secret, keep it to yourself. But sometimes you just have to confide in someone to relieve stress and regain peace of mind. Sometimes revealing a secret to a trusted friend, and receiving the benefit of his or her counsel, is just plain necessary. When friends share with us in confidence an important part of their life that they do not want anyone but us to know, we must honor the trust implicit in their action and not betray their confidence. Close friends have very few secrets from each other. They are able to share almost everything in confidence, because they are able to trust.

*G*od can make us trustworthy to fully share in our friends' lives and support them.

O LORD, thou hast searched me, and known me.
Thou knowest my downsitting and mine uprising,
thou understandest my thought afar off.
Thou compassest my path and my lying down,
and art acquainted with all my ways.
For there is not a word in my tongue,
but, lo, O LORD, thou knowest it altogether.

PSALM 139:1-4 KJV

Friends Intercede with God for Each Other

*Let such as love Your salvation say continually,
"The LORD be magnified!"*

PSALM 40:16 NKJV

*R*achel, Cloe, and Michelle worked in the same department. They had been hired at about the same time and had become fast  friends. Unlike Rachel and Cloe, Michelle's spirituality included regular prayer. She frequently talked with her friends openly about praying and the intentions she wanted to see accomplished in her prayers. Rachel and Cloe respected this, although this was not something they were accustomed to doing themselves.

Then one day a crisis arose that affected all three of them: Their department was going to be shut down.

"I have been praying for you two all along," Michelle said, "but not specifically about this. Let's ask God together to help us through this specific problem."

Rachel said, "I don't think I know how to pray anymore. . . ."

"It may be too late," Cloe said.

Michelle took them by the hand and bowed her head. "Heavenly Father," she began. . . . The women felt their spirits lift almost immediately.

*L*et us bring the welfare and cares of our friends to God, praying regularly that they may lead healthy, full, and productive lives.

But let everyone who trusts you be happy;
let them sing glad songs forever.
Protect those who love you
and who are happy because of you.
LORD, you bless those who do what is right;
you protect them like a soldier's shield.

PSALM 5:11-12 NCV

Friends Help Protect
Our Good Name

❧

He will rescue me from these liars
who are so intent upon destroying me.

PSALM 57:3 TLB

❧

Alice's promotion to vice president provoked a lot of "water-cooler" discussion. She had worked hard and produced results for her division, and the promotion was not a surprise.

Though the "water-cooler" commentary was generally favorable, the green-eyed monster, jealousy, consumed a few malcontents. They had done nothing noteworthy themselves, but it galled them to see someone else get ahead.

"Alice was a brownnose," one said, snickering, "I guess it finally paid off."

"Alice will do anything to get ahead," one of her so-called friends acknowledged.

"That's not true, and you know it," Stacey said, interrupting them. "I can't believe you guys!"

"Yeah, well, you're her good buddy," said one.

"No, I am her friend, and I'm just telling it how it is," Stacey said.

Friends have the courage and resolve to speak the truth and defend each other. In this, we receive grace and inspiration from God.

Without the help of the LORD
it is useless to build a home
or to guard a city.
It is useless to get up early
and stay up late
in order to earn a living.
God takes care of his own,
even while they sleep.

PSALM 127:1-2 CEV

Friends Walk in Each Other's Shoes

Lord, all my desire is before You;
And my sighing is not hidden from You.

PSALM 38:9 NKJV

Terry could picture Alexis getting ready for the appointment. She would be tense but controlled. She would be focusing on a positive outcome and praying for help. After checking to make sure the doors and windows were safely locked, she would walk into the garage and start the car. Then she would put it in park and go back inside to make

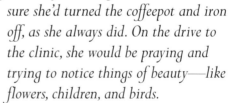

sure she'd turned the coffeepot and iron off, as she always did. On the drive to the clinic, she would be praying and trying to notice things of beauty—like flowers, children, and birds.

And underneath it all, she would be scared to death.

Terry was pained that her friend had to go through this ordeal. She had talked to her late last night and again early this morning, reassuring her and consoling her. She made her promise to call her as soon as she returned even though the results of the biopsy would take a week to come back. Terry would be there for her friend all week long, cheering and encouraging her.

Good friends truly identify with each other and participate in one another's joys and trials. We feel what the other feels, as God does, for all of us.

If I take the wings of the morning
and settle at the farthest limits of the sea,
even there your hand shall lead me,
and your right hand shall hold me fast.
If I say, "Surely the darkness shall cover me,
and the light around me become night,"
even the darkness is not dark to you;
the night is as bright as the day,
for darkness is as light to you.

PSALM 139:9-12 NRSV

Friends Have High Claims on Our Heart

Guard me as the apple of your eye.
Hide me in the shadow of your wings.

PSALM 17:8 NLT

---

*P*age had been planning her summer trip to Europe for two years. She was going on a tour with a group of other accountants, so she would have plenty of familiar company. She had budgeted and scheduled precisely, and had saved hundreds of dollars on nonrefundable airline tickets and hotel accommodations. This was a dream come true. She had only recently paid off her college loans and moved up enough in her career to afford it.

Then three days before Page was to leave from Kennedy Airport in New York, her dear friend Cora's mother and father died in a car accident. The family was devastated. Cora had high-school-age sisters still living at home. It was the end of the world for them and Cora . . . their grief and shock were unimaginable.

Without hesitation, Page canceled her dream trip and raced to Cora's side. Cora would need help with funeral arrangements; she and her younger sisters were in need of tremendous consolation. There was no question in Page's mind about the right thing to do.

---

*S*acrifice is a quintessential aspect of friendship. We can expect it and welcome it, even as God sacrificed His own Son that we should live.

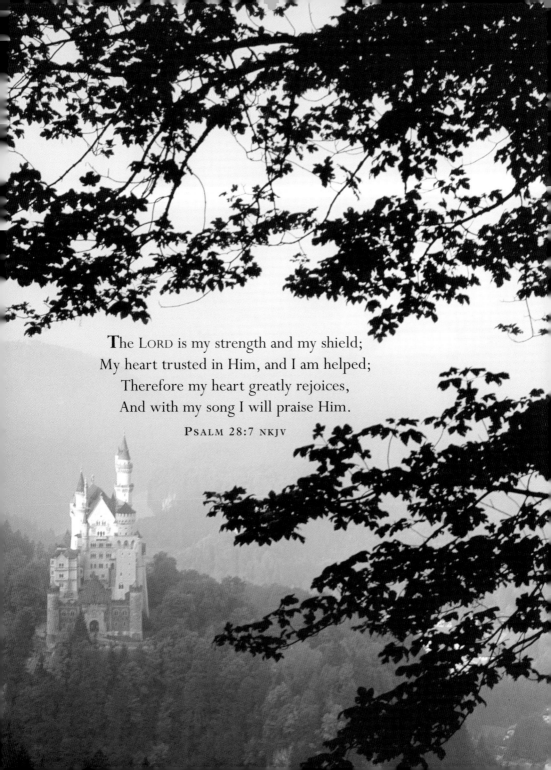

The LORD is my strength and my shield;
My heart trusted in Him, and I am helped;
Therefore my heart greatly rejoices,
And with my song I will praise Him.

PSALM 28:7 NKJV

Friends Survive Tough Tests
of the Relationship

*N*othing stings like the betrayal of a friend. In the Psalms, David often refers to the ill treatment he received from friends and relatives when he was down on his luck. His hurt and disappointment were profound. According to a strict definition of the word, such people were not real friends. They were fakes—fair-weather friends.

It is sometimes hard to stand by our friends when they are foolish and inconsiderate. And it is hard to work through the bitter disappointment when friends let us down. Trust is the essence of friendship; once that is broken, it is difficult to mend. And yet people are flawed; only God is perfect. People may mean well, but they slip and fall somewhere between intention and execution.

This is why we must make God our ideal in matters of love and friendship. We inevitably will fail now and then, in attempting to conform to His fidelity; but by keeping Him clearly before us, we will far surpass the kind of friend we could be on our own.

*W*e must be ready with the necessary strength and stamina to overcome the tough tests of friendship. We can take inspiration from God's example to be agents of His love in the world.

Let me be reconciled
with all who fear you and know your decrees.

PSALM 119:79 NLT

You made me; you created me.
Now give me the sense to follow your commands.
May all who fear you find in me a cause for joy,
for I have put my hope in your word.

PSALM 119:73-74 NLT

Friends Are Allies

The steps of good men are directed by the Lord.
He delights in each step they take.

PSALM 37:23 TLB

Just as God helps us every day of our lives, so we need the help of friends and are obligated to help them in return.

How often news stories chronicle bizarre and tragic crimes committed by people termed "loners." And medical news is peppered with studies about the importance of social support—that is, friends—to personal health. No man is an island. None of us can prosper and thrive without the comfort and assistance of friends. A person alone is deprived of a vital ingredient to life and can be expected to wither and atrophy.

Take a moment to examine your friendship skills. Do you reach out to others? Are you friendly? Do you have others' sincere interests at heart? Are you loyal and affectionate to the friends you already have? Do you know someone who is lonely and needs a friend? If so, do

something about it right now. Pick up the phone and call him or her just to say "hello."

Reaching out to others is not only an obligation but also a source of grace and satisfaction. And the more we use our friendship skills, the better they will be.

The teachings of the LORD are perfect;
they give new strength.
The rules of the LORD can be trusted;
they make plain people wise.

PSALM 19:7 NCV

❧

You give me a better way to live,
so I live as you want me to.

PSALM 18:36 NCV

Friends Are Fellow Pilgrims

Give your burdens to the Lord.
He will carry them.

PSALM 55:22 TLB

Sometimes we forget that our lives are only a prelude to a greater life to come. We are on our way, with every breath we draw, to full and complete fellowship with God, where all our restlessness and troubles will vanish.

In a very real sense we are pilgrims in the here and now, seeking after the face of God. This is the longing that underlies all our

strivings. We desperately need and want to walk with God and draw near to Him every moment.

We should keep this truth foremost in our minds at all times as we go about our earthly business and interact with our friends. Whatever aids and abets our quest for God is good; anything that diverts us from the path is bad and a waste of time.

It is important that we realize our friends are fellow pilgrims with us on our journey to God.

As we fumble about and grope for God, let us take care not to get lost. Let us always keep in mind the prize we are reaching for and encourage our friends to do the same.

Teach me to do thy will;
for thou art my God: thy spirit is good;
lead me into the land of uprightness.
Quicken me, O LORD, for thy name's sake:
for thy righteousness' sake
bring my soul out of trouble.

PSALM 143:10-11 KJV

Friends Plead Our Case

God, your love is so precious!
You protect people in the shadow of your wings.

PSALM 36:7 NCV

$\mathcal{A}$ member of a large church congregation had surgery to repair a misaligned shoulder. It was a simple procedure that was supposed to last only an hour. The man's wife and children, as well as a few members of the church, were at the hospital waiting for the physician to emerge and tell them everything was all right.

Imagine their shock and terror when he arrived to tell them, instead, that the man's heart had stopped on the operating table because of an allergic reaction to the anesthesia. He was legally dead.

The church members flew into action and in a very short time contacted the entire congregation. In unison they prayed for their friend and fellow pilgrim, pleading to God for the man's life and spiritual well-being.

When the man left the operating room he was very much alive.

$\mathcal{G}$od works miracles like this every day when we pray for our friends.

Hear me speedily, O L<small>ORD</small>:
my spirit faileth: hide not thy face from me,
lest I be like unto them that go down into the pit.
Cause me to hear thy lovingkindness in the morning;
for in thee do I trust:
cause me to know the way wherein I should walk;
for I lift up my soul unto thee.

P<small>SALM</small> 143:7-8 <small>KJV</small>

Friends Are Soul Mates

He made their hearts and understands everything they do.

PSALM 33:15 NCV

Terra and Gaye were like sisters. They shared and participated in each other's lives, to the degree that it wasn't always possible to know where one left off and the other began. They had grown up together in the same small southern town where everyone knew them and they knew everyone. Their families worshiped at the same tiny white frame church.

When the time came to go to college, they both went to the state university two hundred miles away and roomed together. Their relationship was based on years of shared memories and an unflinching trust and understanding of each other.

Away from the greenhouse environment of their tiny hometown, life started throwing surprising and sometimes frightening challenges at them. They were startled, stretched, and occasionally threatened by these new experiences. Their minds were engaged and enlarged by a wealth of new information and bold ideas. And through it all, because of the wonderful blessing of friendship, they had each other.

We thank God for our friends. He will help us to be the kind of friend who stands by and endures, the kind of friend who accepts and loves others for who and what they are.

With my whole heart I have sought You;
Oh, let me not wander from Your commandments!
Your word I have hidden in my heart,
That I might not sin against You!

PSALM 119:10-11 NKJV

Friends Care About the Things We Care About

*J*eb's new Lab puppy wandered off one afternoon before he got home from school. Unable to find him anywhere around the house, Jeb went from door to door in the neighborhood, looking for him and putting out the alert that his puppy was loose. Other kids joined in the hunt and fanned out in a half-mile radius from Jeb's house, checking every possible spot a puppy could hide. Parents who were home telephoned others in the neighborhood, and some even got into their cars and slowly cruised the area, looking for the lost puppy.

Jeb was distraught, but surprised and gratified that his neighbors and friends had so much compassion for his plight. He felt certain the puppy would turn up; he just hoped he hadn't been hurt or stolen.

After night fell, most felt that looking for a black puppy in the dark was fruitless and suggested they call off the search until morning. Disappointed, Jeb dragged himself back home. When he walked in the door, he heard his mother calling him.

"Jeb! I found the puppy, honey! He was under the bed!"

Jeb went to sleep that night with his puppy and a newfound sense of the loving community surrounding and supporting him.

*W*e care about our friends and open our hearts to their concerns and problems. We lend a hand and offer hope wherever it is needed.

The LORD looks from heaven;
He sees all the sons of men.
From the place of His dwelling He looks
On all the inhabitants of the earth;
He fashions their hearts individually;
He considers all their works.

PSALM 33:13-15 NKJV

I will extol you, my God and King,
and bless your name forever and ever.
Every day I will bless you,
and praise your name forever and ever.
Great is the LORD, and greatly to be praised;
his greatness is unsearchable.

PSALM 145:1-3 NRSV

Friends Share Each Other's Burdens

I was very worried,
but you comforted me and made me happy.

PSALM 94:19 NCV

---

*E*llen's mother was old and infirm, and although she still lived by herself, Ellen knew the time was coming when her mother would have to move in with her. Her mother was very independent and determined that she did not want to burden her family. Even so, Ellen worried about her all the time, consistently visiting her home across the street two or three times a day.

Ellen's friends were aware of the stress she was feeling and often accompanied her on her visits. They would bring her mother casseroles and tasty desserts and entertaining magazines. It became evident, though, that her mother was in need of more supervision and help; and Ellen feared that a terrible accident might happen before she could get her to the safety of her care at home.

Ellen's friends came to her rescue, though. Over several months, they gently persuaded her mother to move in by insisting that nothing would make Ellen happier.

---

*T*hrough our friends God ministers to us in marvelous ways. Often friends are the means by which He answers our ardent and desperate prayers.

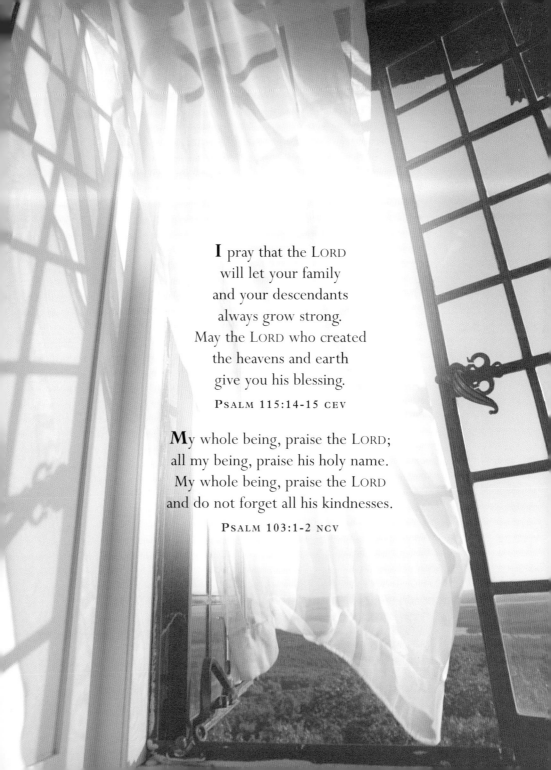

I pray that the LORD
will let your family
and your descendants
always grow strong.
May the LORD who created
the heavens and earth
give you his blessing.

PSALM 115:14-15 CEV

My whole being, praise the LORD;
all my being, praise his holy name.
My whole being, praise the LORD
and do not forget all his kindnesses.

PSALM 103:1-2 NCV

Friends Love the Things We Love

I am a companion of all those who fear You,
And of those who keep Your precepts.

PSALM 119:63 NKJV

$\mathcal{B}$onnie had a close circle of women friends. They all raised their children together, helping one another along the way, sharing secrets, wishes, and dreams. At last their children became young adults and were out of the house living independently. It seemed Bonnie and her friends would be embarking on a new chapter in their lives. New careers, travel, volunteer work . . . and more beckoned.

Then Bonnie came home from her doctor one day with startling news: She was going to have another baby. A host of conflicting feelings crashed over her. She was nearly fifty! She was embarrassed and elated, saddened and overjoyed all at once. Her friends rallied round her and were sympathetic and supportive. They convinced her she was not in this alone—this child would be everyone's baby, loved and looked after by all. They threw Bonnie a marvelous baby shower. And true to their word, when the baby arrived, everyone pitched in and doted on her as if she were their own.

$\mathcal{A}$s best friends, we embrace each other's lives wholly and partake in the love and devotion our friends have for others. In so doing, we become brothers and sisters in God's love and care for the world.

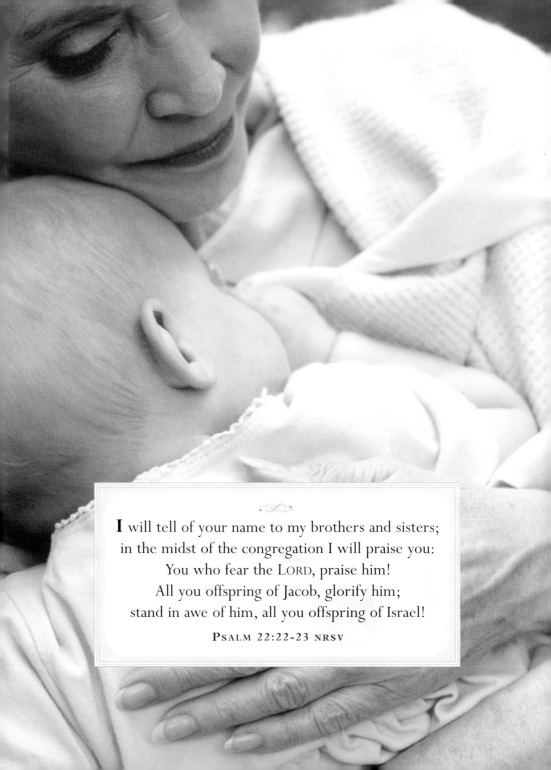

I will tell of your name to my brothers and sisters;
in the midst of the congregation I will praise you:
You who fear the LORD, praise him!
All you offspring of Jacob, glorify him;
stand in awe of him, all you offspring of Israel!

PSALM 22:22-23 NRSV

Friends Abide in the Lord

I entreated Your favor with my whole heart;
Be merciful to me according to Your word.
PSALM 119:58 NKJV

A church setting and the presence of friends sanctify the major events of our lives. Events such as births, baptisms, weddings, promotions, acquiring new homes, and funerals are milestones in life and require an abundance of grace and communal support.

Never miss an opportunity to offer prayer and support for friends when one of these occasions arises. It not only validates and reaffirms your friendship, but is also an essential participation in the life of the mystical body of Christ. Blessings flow all around to friends who gather in acknowledgment and celebration of key transitions in an individual friend's life.

Our lives begin and end with God; a life well lived abides in Him every step of the way. We want the best for ourselves and for our friends, and know that the best can only be found in God.

*W*e commit ourselves to this principle every day and rejoice in the special occasions when we can unite in God's presence to ask His blessings on us.

Show me the path where I should go, O Lord;
point out the right road for me to walk.
Lead me; teach me;
for you are the God who gives me salvation.
I have no hope except in you.

PSALM 25:4-5 TLB

Friends Laugh Together

Oh, give thanks to the LORD, for He is good!
For His mercy endures forever.

PSALM 118:1 NKJV

"What's so funny?" Casey's friend Ann was suddenly choking on laughter. They were talking on the phone, and nothing she had said struck Casey as funny.

"Oh!" Ann gasped, "Sorry! Hold on. . . ." She put the phone down, and her footsteps on the hardwood floor trailed off. . . .

Casey looked at her watch.

"Oh, it's too much," Ann said breathlessly when she returned. "You know how Ed is about the kids getting in his stuff?"

"Yeah," Casey chuckled. Ann's husband had to have everything just so; he was a real neatnik. Everyone teased him about it from time to time. A piece of lint in the wrong place could drive him over the edge.

"The kids have his golf clubs spread all over the backyard. I saw the dog running off with his driver in his mouth."

"Oh no!" Casey shouted.

Ann whooped with laughter. "I gotta run, kiddo!"

When we and our friends are paralyzed by laughter, we are reaping one of the great blessings God gives friends: the honesty possible only among friends.

Truly my soul waiteth upon God:
from him cometh my salvation.
He only is my rock and my salvation;
he is my defence;
I shall not be greatly moved.

PSALM 62:1-2 KJV

The voice of the Lord echoes from the clouds.
The God of glory thunders through the skies.
So powerful is his voice; so full of majesty.

PSALM 29:3-4 TLB

Friends Share Memories

Return to your rest, O my soul,
For the LORD has dealt bountifully with you.
PSALM 116:7 NKJV

*O*ne of the great pleasures of friendship is visiting together the treasury of memories built up over time. When an experience, good or bad, has been shared with a friend it becomes something valuable and serves to bind the friends closer together. Their lives become established conjointly on a firm foundation, and their allegiance and affection for one another grow stronger. The words "Remember when". . . become a familiar and warm prelude to recounting a story of lives shared and the world overcome. Unstated, perhaps, are the words "You were there for me and I was there for you". . . . And may it always be thus.

As we grow older, the memories mount, and the satisfaction friends receive from visiting them together increases. These memories are validating evidence of God's grace at work in our lives. They are proof that we exist and matter in an often seemingly impersonal universe.

*T*hank God for the wonderful blessings of our friends. In them we find His love, purpose, and direction.

From east to west,
the powerful LORD God
has been calling together
everyone on earth.

PSALM 50:1 CEV

Friends Are a Source of Grace for Each Other

*For He satisfies the longing soul,
And fills the hungry soul with goodness.*

PSALM 107:9 NKJV

In a wrenching twist of fate, Emma's husband's business went under the same month her daughter announced she wanted to marry her longtime boyfriend. Emma had always dreamed of a large church wedding with a lovely reception for her only girl. Now she had been hit with a double whammy: serious financial consequences for their family as well as no resources to celebrate her daughter's big day. Emma's friends at church learned of the family's misfortune. Emma had always been extremely generous and giving, and it hurt them to see her in this situation. So they decided to get together and make matters right. Everyone chipped in time and energy to organize a traditional wedding ceremony with a beautiful reception following at the local women's club. Invitations were printed and sent out. A gorgeous dress just the right size was found. The couple took their wedding vows in a church packed with well-wishers and true friends.

Our friends are a favored source for the flow of God's love and blessings to us.

The steps of the godly are directed by the LORD.
He delights in every detail of their lives.
Though they stumble, they will not fall,
for the LORD holds them by the hand.

PSALM 37:23-24 NLT

Friends Are a Shield Against Evil

$\mathcal{T}$ina was short on her tax deposits for the year and worried because she hadn't set the money aside to settle up on April 15. If she had to, she could sell some stock or one of her many fine antiques she had been collecting for nearly twenty years. She was talking this over with Noreen, her tennis buddy, after they finished a set.

"I hate to think of selling anything," she said frowning. "Next year should be a good year for the market, and my antiques are irreplaceable. They've taken me a lifetime to aquire."

Noreen nodded somberly. "It's a tough decision," she agreed.

"I was thinking of not reporting some cash transactions so I could come in even and not have to sell anything," Tina said in a whisper. "Who'd be the wiser?"

"You would, Tina," Noreen said, grimly. "You and You-Know-Who," she said, pointing her finger to the blue sky overhead.

$\mathcal{A}$s a friend, we must be capable of tough love. God wants us to care for our friends as much as He does, and that means pointing out when they are in the wrong.

Turn from evil and do good,
and you will live in the land forever.
For the LORD loves justice,
and he will never abandon the godly.
He will keep them safe forever,
but the children of the wicked will perish.

PSALM 37:27-28 NLT

Friends Are Pleasing in the Eyes of the Lord

Let the favor of the LORD our God be upon us.

PSALM 90:17 NRSV

*F*riendship is a dynamic thing. It doesn't stay still, it is always moving, forming, and reforming according to the circumstances and changes of our lives. Friendship is an active, lively process in which people unite and ally themselves with one another to do the work of the Lord. We involve ourselves in the care of others whom we call our friends and become spiritual brothers or sisters. Like God, we are always there for them, ready to answer when they call on us for help; and ready and willing to help even if they don't consciously think they need—or want—our help, much less our advice.

This is how it should be. From the beginning, according to Genesis, God did not intend for us to be alone in this world. Instead, He gave us soulful companions to help us handle the strife and toil of life. He wanted to bestow on us one of the greatest blessings known to mankind—the joy and comfort derived from true friendship.

*I*f we allow Him to, God will bless all our friends and the ties that bind us together. He will unite us in His love and teach us to be committed to one another.

I will sing of the mercies of the LORD for ever:
with my mouth will I make known
thy faithfulness to all generations.
For I have said,
mercy shall be built up for ever:
thy faithfulness shalt thou establish in the very heavens.

PSALM 89:1-2 KJV

He has given me a new song to sing,
a hymn of praise to our God.
Many will see what he has done and be astounded.
They will put their trust in the LORD.

PSALM 40:3 NLT

This and other books in the Psalms Gift Edition™ series are
available from your local bookstore.

Lighthouse Psalms
Garden Psalms
Love Psalms
Friendship Psalms
Psalms for Women

If you have enjoyed this book, or if it has impacted your life, we
would like to hear from you.
Please contact us at:

Honor Books
Department E
P.O. Box 55388
Tulsa, Oklahoma 74155

Or by e-mail at info@honorbooks.com